Cigarettes & Fortune Tellers

By: Aine Geraghty

Aine Geraghty

ISBN: 0692331743
ISBN-13: 9780692331743

DEDICATION

To my grandfathers.
I'll meet you on the other side.

ACKNOWLEDGMENTS

Thank you to my parents and siblings for truly making my house a home. Thank you to the Colonie Central High School English department for putting up with me.
Thank you to Alana and Mikeisha for constantly showing me a disgusting amount of love and support.
Thank you to everyone who ever had my back.

A Promise

Come with me

To the sea

And inhale

The Ocean's song

If we stay out

Late enough

The mermaids

Will come along.

Java

Sitting there
In that coffee shop
That smelled of Woodstock,
Hot chocolate
Separating our hands,
I wanted to be cold
To you.
I wanted to hate you
So very badly.
I couldn't stand how
Your eyes heated
Like the hazelnut air
When I spoke,
Or how you left
My chest roasted
From your
Complete attention.
But you kept apologizing
For my sadness,
Even though
I promised
It was my fault,
And then I knew
I could never cure
Myself of you.
And truthfully,
I kind of like
The stain you left.

<u>Papa</u>

My latest memory of us
Is a card game
Played on the breakfast table
Upon my arrival home
From a walk
Where things seemed
Hopeless.
My earliest memory of us
Is a late evening in May
Sat in my kitchen,
Still dressed
In annoyingly lovable
Sunflower wallpaper,
Where we blew out
Birthday candles
That weren't ours
To wish on.
If we had those wishes now,
I'd have to blow them away
For the both of us,
And all I would ask for
Would be
One last shuffle of the deck
In our favor.

Cemetery Queen

The cemetery queen,
Dead at seventeen,
Only wakes up
On Halloween.

She asks the skeletons for kisses,
And the corpses about their missus,
Always stopping to pet
Any black cat that hisses.

She dances in crumbling tombs
To songs with a haunting gloom,
Waking the spirits
From their coffined rooms.

Witches love her charm,
Werewolves never do her harm,
And all the young vamps
Leave her hickies up her arms.

Grave circumstances put her in the ground,
But after her burial she was crowned.
Now she is the ghoulish girl
That makes every heart pound.

Seagull Tears

If the sea asked me

To come away,

I know I could drift out

Into the tides

Of faraway possibilities

Because I'm no longer

Anchored here.

That is the thought

That soaks

My pillow

Each evening.

Hopeless

My mother told me

Jesus saves

So I stopped praying

Yesterday.

Because good intentions

Always turn for the worst

And God

Can't help me

For I am cursed.

Gravel

Between the sidewalk

And the street

That is where

Our fates

Finally meet,

With lampposts guiding

My thoughts to you

As wandering souls

Pass right on through.

I'm sitting here

On the curb,

In a place

Where none disturb

My serendipitous gaze

Back into

Our vernal days.

Birthday

It wasn't until

I was standing

With tears in my eyes

Before a freezer

Filled with cakes,

In a grocery store

At three in the morning,

That I understood

Why I didn't want

To celebrate anymore.

The Neighbors

They always smelled like cigarettes

And never forgot my birthday.

I miss that.

Time

Time is a wondrous thing,

Sinking it's roots

Deep into wanderers' minds,

Reminding them

They may have anything

But not everything.

It lines our skin

Like winter jackets

And burns our hearts

With flames of youth.

Time will love us,

Just as it has loved others,

Until it takes us away,

Letting us part from earthly homes

With silenced breaths.

Time will decide the stop

And the start

But we will decide

The journey,

So I'm glad

To have taken it

With you.

Quality

I tried to write

A poem about you,

But it came out

Like store brand cereal;

A cheap knockoff

That just couldn't

Compare.

Allison

With a snip of your thread, you unraveled in my hands

And within a moment, you blew away like the sands

Of time I should have spent by your side.

My steps away from you were steps that I lied.

Come back to my voice and my embrace

For my chest is caving as I kiss your cold face.

How am I supposed to do this without you?

Without that dangerous smile and your cheeks' rosy hue?

I want to finish things for us, for your brave heart

To put things back together, though they are falling apart.

But my last glances of your figure are in black,

Infecting my wounded desire to have your color back.

You were the strong one, you were the fighter.

If only I were strong enough to grip you tighter

To keep you from drifting out into that lost sea

But you were my anchor, and now there's nothing holding you to

me.

Happiness and Lightning

I wish I could show you

How to illuminate

The raging skies

But you're too afraid

To look past the storm.

Take Care Of Me

The lights will go out
And I will cry
With your hand on my chest
Holding my pieces
Together.
You will breathe
For the both of us
Filling my lungs
With midnight honey;
Sweet, warm, binding
And arriving just as time
Has decided to start over.
Then you will rock me
In arms like waves
Tied to the moon
And you will say
"I'll hold you until the tears stop
And then a little longer.
Because I know that's what you want.
I know that's what you need."
And then I'll drift off in your tide
Peacefully drowning
In
Us.

Love Me Not

I'm a flower

Starting to wither,

So I ask you

If I'm still

Worth watering.

But you don't listen.

You just keep saying

"I don't love you."

While plucking

My petals out

One

By

One.

High School Vampires

They don't know about

That home we made

Under the bleachers.

They don't have

Anything as cool

As your switchblade.

They don't like that

We smile in the dark

And come unprepared

To Gym.

But we don't mind.

We're already

Too dead

To care.

Kissing

It was slow

Like waves

In the morning sea.

I felt all of you.

I felt your hands

Cupping my elbows

As if you were catching

Warm summer rain.

I felt the air

Rushing to fill your lungs

And I felt your heart

Knocking at my chest.

It was your lips

I felt the most though.

There really isn't anything

To describe them

Because in reality

They were just lips,

But they were your lips

And that

Made all the difference.

Shed Some Light

We were so good,
Always tumbling and intertwining
Like shirt sleeves
In the washer.
You couldn't help yourself
And I didn't bother
To resist.
But with the sunrise
Came our fall out.
You waited
By my side,
With moonlight
Dripping from your eyes,
As the illuminated tide rose
And seeped
Into memories
Becoming more transparent
With each minute.
We clung to each other
Like static in the winter,
While I prayed
For you to stay,
To stop leaving bits of me
In every small argument
Or jealous dispute
Until I had nothing
Left to love.
Suddenly
I felt the blaze
Veiling me
In a white radiance
And I cried out for you
Only to hear
My echoed call
Of a name
That now brought
A melancholy pang
To my chest.
With the adjustment
Of my eyes
To a brighter world,
Everything seemed
A shade darker.

Deadly Flower Child

Something awoke in me,
Some impish gypsy,
Searching to fit
In my skin
Like a twilight mistress,
Fighting to take me over,
To own my body
Now newly alive.
She sashayed up my spine
And locked into the gaze
Of your eyes,
Burning low
Like a gas stove
Waiting
For a match to drop.
She wanted
To consume you,
To hold your attention
For every remaining hour
You had to live,
So she gave control
Of my stolen figure
To the scream of
The wild summer saxophone
And waited for you
To bite.

Ode To Summer

An ember glow crawls above the horizon
Sneaking in windows on rays of sparkling air
As young minds stir and begin to awaken
With the flutter of eyelids and the tangle of hair.
The early conversations of hounds begin to arise
Along with the pound of sneakers on the street,
While children marinade in elixirs to ward away flies
And lotions to protect from the sun and heat.
What a time for adventurous hearts to grow,
To be swallowed by thick winds and dirt
Where hopes are high and tides are low.

You are a heartbreaker but a promise keeper,
Weaving little patches of happiness into brief kisses of sunshine
In order to make my love for you deeper.
Taking my hand at a quarter to nine,
You walk me through blankets of sand,
While calling to waves that caress my feet
And dropping salty sprinkles on skin thats tanned.
Your touch is so bittersweet.
I know I can't keep you, and you know it too
But you bring me such life with your blazing presence
That I end up spending all my time enjoying the view.

Leaving nothing but ice-cream stains on the drive
And solace in faded photos of the sea,
You vanish to make others feel alive
So I am greeted with an embrace much more icy.
You say you'll be back, but what if I don't make it there?
Will you hold me forever in a new place?
I'd like to think you would, but you probably don't care
You get around quite often and I'm just another face.
If I Fall during this absence of your warmth and ecstasy
Will you promise to resurrect me like the foliage
And always love me?

Passing

You left

Without a reason

In the world.

I'd say you

Couldn't imagine

The pain I felt,

But your heart

Gave out too,

So i'm sure

You could.

Beetles On The Windowsill

Little children

Wander

With backpacks

That glimmer

Like overpriced

Gasoline murals

In vacant

Parking lots.

Cat Power

Plays softly,

Generating an anthem

For dandelion seeds

In the wind,

And as my eyes

Grow heavy

Following the infinite patterns

Of their tiny legs,

I wonder

If there is any use

Wishing to be

Somewhere else.

Home Insurance

We are all little houses

Throwing stones at each other

Trying to break windows.

We lock our doors,

Light our fires

And watch all the other homes,

Hoping their roofs cave in

Or their pipes burst.

But in this time

Smoke fills our rooms

From flames we left unattended

While we glared at our neighbors.

Now the fireplaces

Can't hold back the roaring heat

And we helplessly

Try to escape our boarded up homes

As they burn down

Around us.

Mystery Girl

Her name is Stardust.

Yesterday it was Miracle

And tomorrow we just don't know,

But today

She wants to be new.

Right now

She's out on the back porch

In knee high socks

And a peach sweater,

Smoking a Menthol

While her bare thighs

Stick to the wet stones.

She does this every morning,

And I'm afraid

To ask why,

For the answer may be

Far different than

What we'd like to hear.

Brain Instrumental

Deep within
My tired mind
There is a place
By the sea.
It is always
Midnight there,
Cloaking the water
In a dark calm.
When I go
I walk the boardwalk,
Deserted by those
Whose dreams don't
Haunt them.
Sitting down
On the edge,
I watch the mermaids
Play below my feet
And I look for
The pirate ship
That is always sitting
On the horizon
Where the Moon melts
Into the waves.
This enchanting scene
Never changes.
It remains the same
In the hopes that
I will return again.
And I always do
Find my way back
Because my thoughts
Are quiet there.

Slayer

You're my slumber party massacre,

All wrapped up in

Bad decisions

And bloody good times.

I want to cruise

Dirty deserted highways

With you,

On the edges

Of darkness,

Hoping we'll find a soul

Unlucky enough to be

Our good time.

Let's keep

Odd hours

Together.

Hopelessly Devoted

Every reason to live

Punched me in the stomach

When you smiled at me

Like you were in love

And even though I knew

That wasn't the case

I decided that lie

Was beautiful enough

To wake me up each day.

Out Of This World

When I make it to the moon

I will send back stars

To all the aliens

That blew me kisses

Along the way,

But I'll feel sorry

For all the others

That said my spaceship

Wouldn't make it there

Because gravity keeps

Holding them back.

Memories

I remember that summer,
With all its stereoscope houses
And foggy mornings.
I remember the bike rides
Down those dirt paths
That ran for miles,
When we had nothing with us
Except flowers
In our hair
And homemade cookies
In our baskets.
I remember how much life
Our dresses had
And how little
We cared about anything.
And I remember now
Why I woke up this morning
Missing you.
You and your garnet hair,
Polaroid smile
And that laugh
That stripped my soul naked
And breathed new life into it.
It was because
I never wanted to
Have to
Remember you.

<u>Myself</u>

I found her,

Giggling in a pillow fort

On the third

Of April,

And she was beautiful

In every sense of the word.

I wonder where

She has run off to

Now.

Growth

I lost the child,

Once a travler

Hitching a ride

To the final memories

Of adolescent ignorance,

But replaced her

With the girl

Who grew

From every failure

Of the heart's

Sincerest beliefs

Into the woman

Without a single

Goddamn thing

Standing in her way.

Reverse It

Whenever I think about

Walking,

My feet tangle

And movement becomes

A foreign concept.

Whenever I think about

How loud I'm

Laughing,

The joke doesn't seem

To tickle my ribs

Quite as much.

Whenever I think about

Smiling,

My teeth feel out of place,

Like they're all wrong

In their alignment.

So,

I just stop.

I wish the same

Were true for when

I think about

How much

I love you.

Remember Us

Leave me a ghostly handprint

On the window

So I know

I still pass by

In your thoughts.

I'll leave you

A lipstick stain

On your pillowcase

So you remember

That I never

Gave up on us.

Let's hope

Someday we get

Another chance

To not fuck it up.

Ghosts

We will meet there,

Where the pink of skin

Matches the flowers

And the air

Sticks my shirt

To my chest

Like a damp hug.

I know you'll

Remember me,

You were always

Good with that stuff,

And no one

Will give a second glance

To the two spirits

Joining hands

In the distance.

A Movie About Honesty

I'm making a short film

That I want you to be in.

It's called

" To Tell You How I Feel".

It's a silent film

And you get stabbed

In the opening scene.

Smooth Sleep Talker

I said

I'm only pretty

In my dreams,

That's why I sleep

So much.

Then you said

I was only beautiful

When you slept,

That's why you haven't

Woken up yet.

Today

You've got me dancing

On the tips of my toes,

Wishing this time

Between the showers

Of glittering dust particles

In the sunrise

And the crashing

Of cotton waves

Over our bodies

Would never end.

Just like my love

For You.

Playmates

Chocolate eyes

And tangled thighs

Swim for hours

Underneath seas of cotton,

While kisses are traded

Like baseball cards

And squeals of laughter

Arise from the nipping

Of ticklish hips.

Let's stay this way

Until this old mattress

Learns our shape.

<u>Forest</u>

I only think of the trees

And how I wish

They would uproot me

From the state of mind

I've been planted in.

I'd like nothing more

Than to live only

In the sun's days

And die

In the winter

Before my heart

Freezes over.

Dependency

I keep telling myself

You aren't my only

Chance for

Happiness,

That I can

Find it

Within

If I try.

But I'm beginning

To think

That's just

A hopeless

Little

Lie.

Bait

You came at me

Like a shark fin

In the middle of the ocean

And the Jaws of life

Had to rip me from you

Once you pulled me

Under the tide.

One would think

I'd stay closer to shore

When I know

I can't swim,

But I can't resist

Your teeth

Sinking into my skin.

Travel

We were naked,

Unafraid to touch

The edge of the world.

With foreheads

Pressed to glass barriers

We gazed down

On lives

We couldn't touch

And watched

The days of skeletons

Drive by.

Ideas crept

In and out

As we parked

In blue moonlight,

The only certain thing

Being our desire

To see it all.

Illuminate

I am not your lamp.

I am not yours

To keep in some dark corner

Of your room

And only use

When you need me

To show the way

So you don't fall.

If I am light

Then I am the stars

Created for many great purposes

Scattered in a million places

But still all together.

My only friends

Being the Moon

And the Universe,

I come and go

On my own time.

And if I so happen

To help guide you,

Then I am glad.

But I'm not

Your fucking lamp.

Michael

The way your Jeep smells
And the way you look
When your driving it
As you blast classic rock.
The way you laugh
At my jokes
And even harder
At your own.
The way your eyes
Remind me of a doe
As you smile
When I talk.
And the way
You treat me,
Like you refuse
To leave me behind.
All of these things
Are the reasons I can't live
Without you.
The reasons I want you.
The reasons I need you.
The reasons I love you.
But they are probably
All the same reasons why
She loves you.
And I'm not dumb,
So I know who
You'll choose.

Engaged

Pillow fights

In the dead of night

That end in

Tender kisses and tickling

Could drive a girl insane.

I'm so lucky

I fell madly

In love with you

Long ago.

Arizona

She dances with the cacti

In the forgotten deserts

Of summer rain.

Her sand laced hair

Weaves itself

Into a mystic story

Down her boney

Shoulders

Until it meets

The hug of denim

At her waist.

Her eyes are like

Moonstones

And her heart is a

Crater

That swallows all those

Who try to fill it.

She is the most

Dangerous blessing

One could ever

Pass by

In a midnight

Dream.

Midnight

Im up late

Playing solitaire on my laptop

While I listen to soft indie music.

You're probably awake too

Reading a mystery novel

Enjoying the silence of a sleeping house.

I think that says

Something.

Unforgiving

Glitter poured from

Her red eyelids,

While she held

A gaze

That glimmered

Like New York City.

She deserved more,

And she knew it.

But she kept thinking

About that cake

He bought

For her last birthday

And the shirts

She borrowed

That he never asked

To have back.

Then she convinced

Herself

She got everything

She deserved.

Damp Soul

The night sea,

Painted with moonlight,

Promised my heart something

I couldn't quite understand.

But I wandered

Through the waves

Like a ghost

Moving toward Heaven

And I never looked back

For the water

Filled a hole

Deep within my chest

Making me,

Just for a little while,

Feel whole again.

Abandoned Library

You have been left,

With windows broken and

Water stained carpeting.

Your doors are now barred

So only the strongest

May break through

And your once enchanting

Glass ceiling

Has shattered from the storms.

But you are still

Beautiful.

You know so much

And you share so little,

Which could fascinate someone

For centuries.

You are a hidden

Attraction

And if one doesn't spend

Eternity discovering

All your little details

Then they have lived

A wasted life.

You are the

Abandoned library.

Knock At My Door

Within this honey field
Time always seems to yield
When you ride by on your bike
And my heartbeat starts to spike.

Sometimes I pretend we walk together
Picking flowers and lost bird feathers
And if you would be so kind to give me a chance
In this private meadow we could dance.

I like to think that one day
You'll knock on my door and ask to stay
And I will take your hand and lead you inside
For my heart and home have nothing to hide.

Even with the rain and snow
Do not think you have to go
I've plenty of blankets and a window to view
The storms outside, cuddled to you.

But all of this is simply a dream
So I'll sit with my feet dipped in this stream
And wait for you to pass once more
My heart still waiting for that knock at my door.

<u>Hands</u>

When you enter

The room,

I stare at my palms

Until my hands

Are not my hand,

Because when I look

At the gaps between

My fingers

And don't find you there

I just don't feel

Like myself anymore.

Paper Love

On the day you told me

The card I had made you

Was hanging

On your wall

I went home and cried

Because

That was the closest

To hearing you say

I love you

I would ever get.

3 A.M.

"I love tunnels.",

She said.

"They're so poetic."

Then she was silent

And I smiled,

Enjoying her thoughts,

While endlessly drifting

Into dreams

Inside the city

That never slept.

The Sun

Blinded by her own rays
She cannot see
Who she is,
So she longs to be
The Moon.
She wishes to sit among the stars
And be gazed at.
She wants to be mysterious,
Revealing only portions of herself
Each evening.
She wants to have control,
To be able to pull the tides
And drown her sorrows.
But she doesn't know
She is something
Just as marvelous.
Her beauty is so great
It is not for mortal eyes
To fully devour.
She brings life
To the flowers
And the people,
Who would wither away
Without her.
And although she is sad
She forgets
She is the symbol of happiness
For so many others
Who simply
Adore her.
If only she knew
She was the brightest
Of all the stars
In the sky.

-To The Sun, Ariane.

www.ingramcontent.com/pod-product-compliance
Lightning Source LLC
Chambersburg PA
CBHW070458050426
42449CB00012B/3028